redefine
LIFE GOD'S WAY

PASTOR RANDAL ROSS
CALVARY CHURCH
NAPERVILLE, ILLINOIS

THE REDEFINE TEAM

EXECUTIVE PRODUCERS:
Randal Ross, Ben De Boef, Kregg Hood, Keith Boucher

WRITERS:
Randal Ross, Kregg Hood

HOSTS:
Alan Krashesky, Milenka Peña

SESSION TEACHERS:
Randal Ross, Alberto López

LEADER LIFTER TEACHERS:
Ben De Boef, Ángel Escamilla

HOST HOMES:
Greg & Debbie Field,
Bill & Sharon Goodwin

MEDIA PRODUCTION:
Sarah Dawes, Dallas Thiele, Dave Sheneman, Tyler Adams, Evan Griffin

ASSISTANTS:
Neria Oyejola, Shellie Wooten, Betty Stewart, Jill Thornton

SPANISH TRANSLATION:
Sandalio Atenco,
Marlene Hernandez

SPANISH PRODUCTION:
Alberto López,
Ángel Escamilla,
Yanira Segarra, Milenka Peña

PHOTOGRAPHERS:
Andrew Barickman, Vicky Cape, Olivia Foster, Kurt Guerrero, David Jackson, Maurice Johnson, Bev Jordan, Steve McCullough, Gil Morgan, Olu Oyejola, Oggie Perez, John Shurtz

redefine
LIFE GOD'S WAY

CONTENTS

APPENDIX

SMALL GROUP LEADERS

ABOUT THE AUTHOR

WHAT OTHERS ARE SAYING

Wayne Blackburn
Senior Pastor, Victory Church, Lakeland, Florida

"*Redefine* is an inspiring tool for anyone seeking truth for daily guidance. It captures comprehension techniques in a small group setting that inspire the seeker to think, adjust, and apply godly truths to their daily lives. Randal Ross has stretched static biblical words toward inspiring, life-changing truths that challenge the imagination."

Dr. Samuel R. Chand
Author, *Cracking Your Church's Culture Code*

"So, you want a totally biblical, pragmatic discipleship resource that comes with a user manual, which is easy to use? Well, look no further. Here it is! *Redefine* by Pastor Randal Ross is the answer for developing disciples who disciple others. Just add water."

Herbert Cooper
Lead Pastor, People's Church, Oklahoma City, Oklahoma

"We are all created with a God-given desire to be successful. Pastor Randal does an outstanding job on helping followers of Christ understand true biblical success!"

Jim Hennesy
Senior Pastor, Trinity Church, Cedar Hill, Texas

"Pastor Ross effectively reclaims from American culture the life-giving principles only available via truth. The messages presented in *Redefine*, lovingly expose the soft underbelly of America's popular promises and replaces them with firm foundations upon which we can build meaningful lives."

Bryan Jarrett
Lead Pastor, Northplace Church, Sachse, Texas

"I find Randal Ross to be a man of impeccable character whose passion for God and people is contagious. This book is a reflection of that charisma and character."

Rick Knoth
Managing Editor, *Enrichment Journal*, The General Council of the Assemblies of God

"*Redefine* is a tour de force among small-group curricula. An important feature of *Redefine*, and one not usually associated with small-group material, is the incorporation of five pedagogical elements to enhance the believer's walk with Christ. Pastor Randal Ross' fresh and practical six-week study examines six key words of Jesus in light of contemporary interpretation. *Redefine* is a great resource for bolstering one's faith and equipping one to live a fully engaged Christian life."

David McQueen
Lead Pastor, Beltway Park Baptist Church, Abilene, Texas

"I was honored to serve on a team that was led by Pastor Ross for almost nine years. The Lord used those nine years to place foundational matters deep within me. These were foundational things I heard Pastor Ross saying and observed him living, the same foundational principles to successful living that he graciously shares in this book. These things have made all the difference in my personal life and in my life as a leader, and I'm confident that they'll do the same for you."

Jim Raley
Senior Pastor, Calvary Christian Center, Ormond Beach, Florida

"Pastor Randal Ross has written an incredible book. With the turning of each page, readers are inspired to view themselves through the eyes of Christ and embrace the fullest life possible. Apply the powerful principles of this book and get ready to live life 'redefined.'"

Jerry Rose
President, Total Living Network

"*Redefine* is a call to Christians for a genuine commitment to Christ that is desperately needed in the Church today. It will be a spiritually transforming force in the lives of those who commit to the study. Thanks, Pastor Ross, for taking the time to make it a reality."

Rick Ross
Lead Pastor, CFA Church, Concord, North Carolina

"If you ask the wrong question, then you will always get the wrong answer. My older brother, Randal, has helped me over the years to ask the right questions. Now, *Redefine* will help you to ask the right questions along your spiritual journey. The practical lessons and group discussions will guide you into experiencing life God's Way."

Gary Smalley
Author, *The DNA of Relationships*

"I personally believe that one of the best things we can do in our walk with the Lord is conduct a complete study on the teachings of Jesus. *Redefine* is a very practical, easy-to-read book that brings the teachings of Scripture to life in a fresh and unique way. What Pastor Ross says will help people realize the benefits of trusting and following God in all aspects of life."

Rich Wilkerson
Lead Pastor, Trinity Church, Miami, Florida

"I have known Pastor Randal Ross for 25 years and have always known him to be a leader and church builder. Not everyone is aware that Pastor Ross is also a discipler of people. In his latest book, *Redefine*, you will be reacquainted with the basics of this Christian walk."

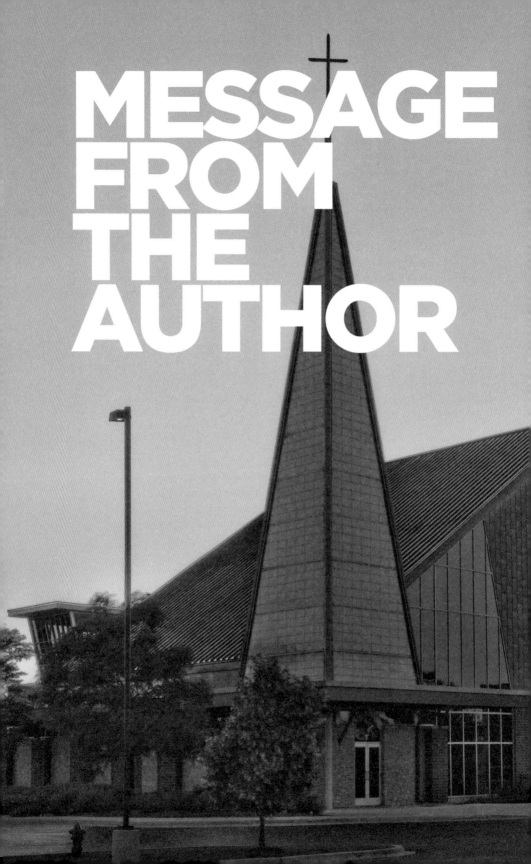

MESSAGE FROM THE AUTHOR

People who hear me regularly know that I often encourage them to read the words in the Bible that are printed in red. That's because, in most of our Bibles, the "red letter" words are the quotations from Jesus. What Jesus actually said is always at the center of where you will find good news. Jesus is truly the source of "good news." He knows how the world should run because, after all, he made it! Jesus lived good news, taught good news, and brought good news as his "A" game every day.

Wherever he went, joy, peace, and healing followed. In fact, the only people who disliked Jesus were the religious phonies and powerbrokers of his day. All they ever did was make life harder and more discouraging for everyone else, so Jesus either ignored them or went around them. He was determined to set people free, and that single-minded focus gave him the motive and the right to show us all a better way.

In this new series, we are going to take a close, intimate look at the personal words of Jesus in his quest to shepherd us away from weak ideas and poor decisions. We're going to take a fresh, practical look at several of his key words on a variety of contemporary needs. Then we will apply them to several common situations today in order to find the better path. In fact, to emphasize the process of this study, we've entitled the series *Redefine*.

As you study, listen, and interact with your friends, prepare to pay close attention to several important words that target a number of significant themes in your life. In every case, each word has been either incorrectly defined or, at the very least, poorly defined. The good news is that, when you allow Jesus to redefine your understanding and your actions, you will also discover ways to help you accomplish key needs in your life.

Sometimes we just get stuck in our thinking. Then, if we don't see all of the truth that we need to see, we miss the answers and blessings that God wants to release into our lives. He is always the ultimate power source, but we have a part to play, too. If you're on the right path, God's way of looking at things will give you greater strength and determination in the future. If you're off track but embrace the redefinitions we will study, you will learn how to re-engage life and take positive action.

Pastor Randal Ross

USING THIS WORK BOOK

1. In the Table of Contents, notice that there are some special sections in the back of this book: "Appendix" and "Small Group Leaders." Familiarize yourself with the "Appendix," which will be referenced in the sessions.

2. If you are facilitating/leading or co-leading a small group, the "Small Group Leaders" section will give you some hard-learned experiences of others that will encourage you and help you to avoid many common obstacles to effective small group leadership.

3. Use this workbook as a guide, not a straightjacket. If the group responds to the lesson in an unexpected but honest way, go with that. If you think of a better question than the next one in the lesson, ask it. Take to heart the insights included in the "Frequently Asked Questions" pages and the "Small Group Leaders" section.

4. Enjoy your small group experience.

5. Read the "Outline for Each Session" on the next pages so that you understand how the sessions will flow.

OUTLINE FOR EACH SESSION

Most people want to live a God-honoring life, but few achieve this by themselves. Most small groups struggle to balance all of God's purposes in their meetings. Groups tend to overemphasize one of the various reasons for meeting. Rarely is there a healthy balance that includes teaching, evangelism, ministry, practical exercises, and worship. That's why we've included all of these elements in this study so that you can live a healthy, balanced spiritual life over time.

A typical group session for *Redefine* will include the following:

INTRODUCTION. Each lesson will open with a brief thought that will help you to prepare for the session and get you thinking about the particular subject that you will explore with your group. Make it a practice to read these before the session.

LISTEN. As in, *listen to God and each other's lives.* The foundation for spiritual growth is an intimate connection with God and his family. A few people who really know you and earn your trust provide a place to experience the life that Jesus invites you to live. This section of each session typically offers you two options. You can get to know your whole group by using the icebreaker question(s), or you can check in with one or two group members—your spiritual partner(s)—for a deeper connection and encouragement in your spiritual journey.

DVD TEACHING SEGMENT. Serving as a companion to the *Redefine* small group discussion book is the *Redefine Video Teaching*. This DVD is designed to combine teaching segments from Pastor Randal Ross, along with leadership insights and personal stories of life change.

Using the teaching video will add value to this six-week commitment of doing life together and discovering how walking with Christ changes everything.

LEARN. This section is where you will process as a group the teaching that you heard and saw. The focus won't be on accumulating information but will be on how we should live in light of the Word of God. We want to help you apply the insights from Scripture practically, creatively, and from your heart as well as your head. At the end of the day, our greatest aim is to allow the timeless truths from God's Word to transform our lives in Christ.

LIVE. In this portion, we let the truth that we are learning travel the eighteen inches from our cranium (mind) to our cardium (heart, emotions, and will). This is where the place in the Bible that instructs us to "be doers of the Word, not just hearers" (James 1:22) comes into play. Many people skip this aspect of the Christian life because it's scary, relationally awkward, or simply too much work for their busy schedules. But Jesus wanted all of his disciples to help outsiders connect with him, know him personally, and carry out his commands. This doesn't necessarily mean preaching on street corners. It could mean welcoming a few newcomers into your group, hosting a short-term group in your home, or walking through this study with a friend. In this study, you'll have an opportunity to go beyond Bible study to biblical living.

LOVING OTHERS/LOVING GOD. As in, *love the Lord your God and your neighbor, too.* We have Jesus' affirmation that every aspect of life's destiny can ultimately be measured as a way of fulfilling one or both of the "bottom line" commandments: "The foremost," answered Jesus, "is, 'Hear, O Israel! The Lord our God is one Lord; and you shall love the Lord your God with all your heart, and with all your soul, and with all your mind, and with all your strength.' The second is this, 'you shall love your neighbor as yourself.' There is no other commandment greater than these" (Mark 12:29–31). The group session will close with time for personal response to God and group prayer, seeking to keep this crucial commandment before us at all times.

GOING DEEPER BIBLE STUDY. If you have time and want to dig deeper into more Bible passages about the topic at hand, we've provided additional passages and questions. Your group may choose to do study homework ahead of each meeting in order to cover more biblical material. If you prefer not to do study homework, the "Going Deeper" section will provide you with plenty to discuss within the group. These options allow individuals or the whole group to expand their study while still accommodating those who can't do homework or are new to your group.

DAILY REFLECTIONS. Each week on the "Daily Reflections" pages, we provide Scriptures to read and reflect on between group meetings. We suggest that you use this section to seek God on your own throughout the week. This time at home should begin and end with prayer. Don't get in a hurry; take enough time to hear God's direction.

WEEKLY MEMORY VERSES. For each session, we have provided a verse that emphasizes an important truth from the session. This is an optional exercise, but we believe that memorizing Scripture can be a vital part of filling our minds with God's will for our lives. We encourage you to give this important habit a try.

SESSION 1
SUCCE

SS

Success is a word that makes you sit up and take notice. I can almost hear a drum roll right now, can't you? We are people who tend to be easily impressed with success. We are enamored with it. Reality TV shows, especially when they feature "successful" people, are the most popular type of program these days. Frankly, since we know there's very little reality in reality shows, perhaps we shouldn't let them shape the way we understand success.

But there *is* something alluring—even magnetic—about success that usually makes us want more of it, maybe even all we can get. I suppose it's because we tend to associate success with wealth, pleasure, and getting our own way. At the same time, we also know that success leads to a huge price, too. Many of us may find that successful people are intimidating, and, while we like the results of their success, we often dislike them and what it has taken for them to be successful. We can see how the unbridled pursuit of success breeds envy and heartache and can even destroy families and friendships.

The good news at the start of our study is that, while lasting success is quite different from what the world emphasizes, God is not against success; he is for success. But he wants us to have the right kind

of success—success that is real, genuine, and empowering. When we let God define success for us and keep our lives out of the ditches, we will experience the results that he has for us. God delights in us right now. That is why success—God's way—is more about whom you are becoming than about what you do. As you become more like Christ, you will discover his special plans for you. Are you willing to look to Jesus for those plans? The journey is worth the effort because the success that Jesus offers is deep and lasting. To know if you are on the right track, start with a look inside your heart. What do you see? If you see a growing sense of humility, a desire to serve and give to others, and a willingness to show kindness and compassion, then you are headed for success. If people matter more to you than your possessions, then you are prepared for more success.

LISTEN

During each session, we begin with a question or brief activity that is designed to put us "on the same page" for the session. Since this is your first time together (at least for this new series), take a few minutes to make sure that everyone knows each other's name.

1. What words come to mind when you hear the word *success*?

2. Describe a variety of events that people often use to illustrate success.

Watch the DVD teaching for this session now. We have provided space for you to take notes on page 28. This is where you can record any key thoughts, questions, and things that you want to remember or follow up on. After watching the video, have someone read the discussion questions in the "Learn" section and direct the discussion among the group. As you go through each of the subsequent sections, ask someone else to read the questions and direct the discussion.

LEARN

These sessions will place special emphasis on the actual words of Jesus in your Bible. Sure, all Scripture is inspired by God (as Paul reminds us in II Timothy 3:16), but the direct words

of Christ add an even more powerful, personal dimension to our study because they take us into the very heart and mind of God. The intimate teaching of Jesus for his disciples reaches across the centuries and arrives in our lives as fresh and transforming as the day the words were spoken. We want his words to become familiar guides as we live our lives. Using the questions that follow, review and expand on the teaching that you just experienced.

"God is

3. Pastor Ross described the goal of these sessions as "redefining or recapturing the great words of doing life." He wants us to not just "know" these words; he wants us to know what they actually mean. What are some of the benefits of using words when we actually know what they mean?

4. At the end of his Sermon on the Mount (Matthew 5–7), Jesus closed with this application point: "Therefore everyone who *hears these words of mine* and puts them into practice is like a wise man who built his house on the rock. The rain came down, the streams rose, and the winds blew and beat against that house; yet it did not fall, because it had its foundation on the rock. But everyone who *hears these words of mine* and does not put them into practice is like a foolish man who built his house on sand. The rain came down, the streams

for success"

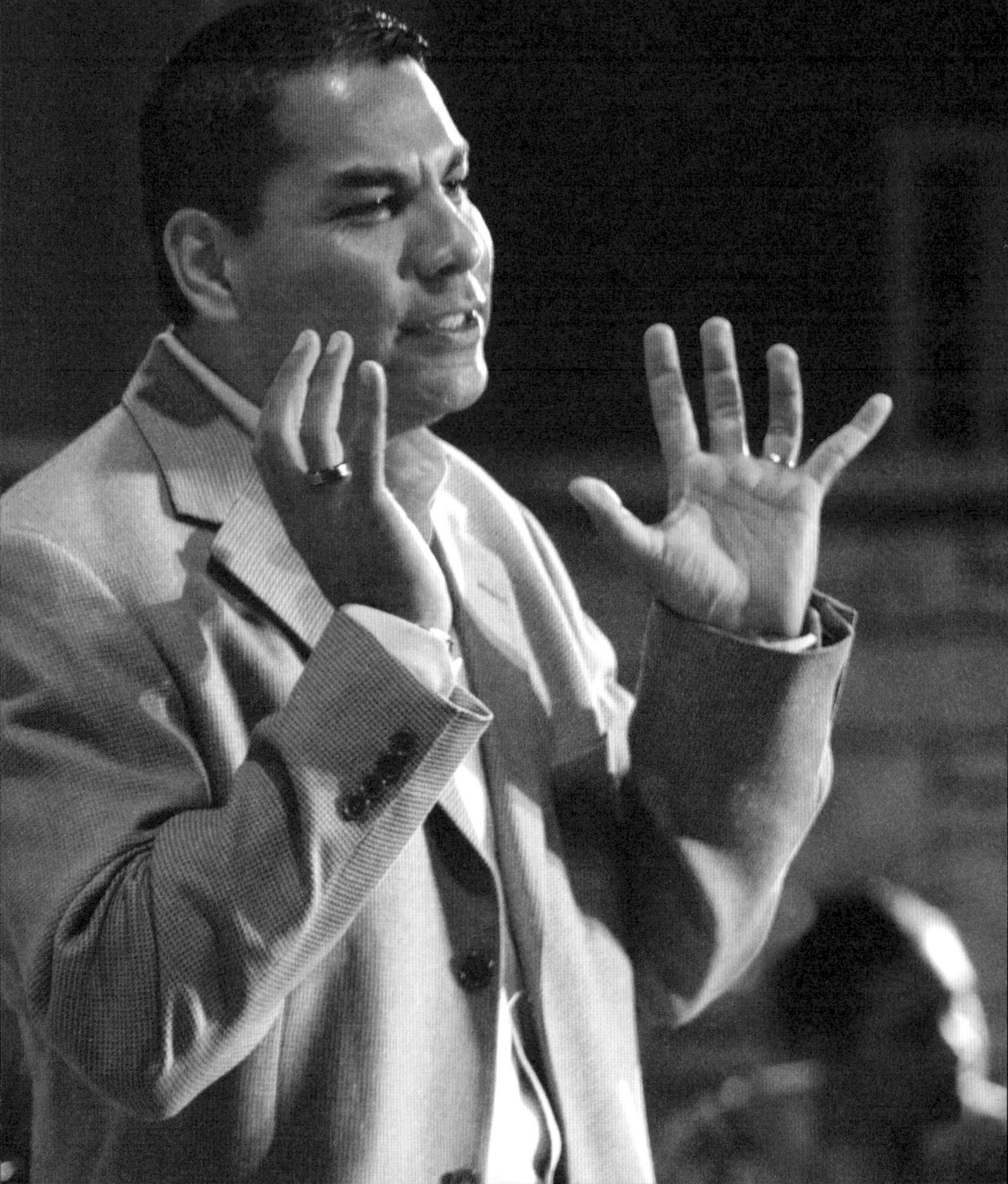

rose, and the winds blew and beat against that house, and it fell with a great crash" (Matthew 7:24–27, italics added).

How did Jesus separate the two kinds of people he knew were listening to his teaching even though both groups "hear(s) these words of mine"?

5. In Jesus' illustration, why is it significant that the same kinds of storms came into the lives of both groups that he described? How does a house standing against terrible weather help us to understand success?

6. How would you explain the difference that Pastor Ross pointed out between the world's definition of success

(lots of stuff, arrival, and place) compared to God's definition of success (journey, process, and becoming)?

7. When you heard the statement, "In fact, the wrong definition of success can ruin your life," how did those words strike you?

8. Pastor Ross defined godly success as "keeping your life on track with God and out of the ditches." What are some ways that we can expand on or explain the two phrases "on track with God" and "out of the ditches"?

"The success

LIVE Now it's time to make some personal applications for everything we've been thinking about over the past few minutes. God's definition of success focuses us on what we're becoming. It is ultimately confirmed by the way we live before God and others. This means that our true destiny is tied to how we bring good to others within our capacities and opportunities. We also know that God gives us wisdom to make the most of our service to him and for others. This is his purpose and plan.

9. Developing our ability to serve God according to the leading of the Holy Spirit takes time and persistence as we get to know our Lord. We must take time in prayer, in God's Word, and in meditation to let God speak to us daily. Again, think of this as your success journey and identify the steps that God wants you to take for the next few weeks. What do you sense is next for you?

Prayer. Commit to personal prayer and daily connection with God. You may find it helpful to write your prayers in a journal.

Reflection. Each session includes "Daily Reflections." This is an opportunity to read a short Bible passage during the week of that session. Write down your insights on what you read each day. On the last day, summarize what God has shown you throughout the week.

Meditation. Try meditation as a way of internalizing God's Word more deeply. Write a portion of Scripture on a card and tape it somewhere in your line of sight, such as your car's dashboard or the kitchen table. Think about it when you sit at red lights or while you're eating a meal. Reflect on what God is saying to you through these words. Several passages for meditation are suggested on the "Daily Reflections" page in each session.

:hat Jesus offers
is deep and lasting."

10. In God's plan, how is success a personal pursuit that can't really be compared with what others are doing? Why is it important to focus on being and doing what God planned specifically for you?

11. What would be easier for you to produce on paper: a "to do" list or a "to be" list? What would be the value of each of them? Why is one more important?

12. Pastor Ross summarized the teaching for this session with this statement: "We can redefine/recapture success God's way. We lived our lives to please him above all others." Explain briefly how you understand this in the light of the lesson.

13. Our hero for this session (see the "Memory Verse") is Joseph who had his share of storms and wind that tried to beat down his house. How was he successful? What pattern or lesson from his life would you like to copy in your own life?

LOVING OTHERS/ LOVING GOD

The success that God has in mind for us will always include others. The more we understand the way that God put us together, the more we can begin to see how he can impact the lives of others through us.

14. What personal implications can you see in the following explanation: Success is not measured by what you achieve but by how many people you take with you on your journey?

15. Since success includes helping others, what decision could you make this week (and share with the group) that you know would be a step toward success in your life?

16. Allow everyone to answer this question: How may we pray for you this week? Be sure to write prayer requests in your "Prayer & Praise" section on page 134.

Close the session in prayer. Pray for others in the group. Use the following prayer as you lean into God:

Heavenly Father, today I choose to follow the path that you have marked out for me. May your will be done in my life. I know that's the path to success. I need your help. Where I am weary, renew my strength. When I am distracted, redirect my attention by your grace. Holy Spirit, help me to recognize anything that hinders my progress. In Jesus' name, Amen.

GOING DEEPER

As a group, you can explore the following Bible passages behind the teaching for this session (if there is time) or on your own between sessions.

Read Luke 12:13-21.

This is a sharp and counter-cultural teaching that Jesus gave on the subject of success and wealth. It includes the warning that apparent blessings from God are not licenses for reckless decision-making.

How did Pastor Ross highlight the contrast in God's eyes between covetousness and success?

How could the rich man in Jesus' parables have handled his windfall in better ways?

What would keep you from handling prosperity in the same way that the rich man in Jesus' parable approached it?

Read Genesis 37, 39-41.

These four chapters describe Joseph's early life and rise to power. They trace his persistence in the light of continual setbacks. A review of his experiences will give you a fresh glimpse of the unimportance of circumstances in the development of success. Those who succeed in God's eyes do so despite their circumstances—good or bad.

In Genesis 39:1-4, what clues caused an Egyptian officer to turn over the management of his estate to a young Jewish slave?

What kinds of obstacles/setbacks did Joseph have to outlive (see Genesis 37:8, 18–20, 26–27; 39:1, 7–9, 11–12, 20; 40:3–4, 14–15, 23)?

Why is perseverance a key component in God's definition of success?

DAILY

REFLECTIONS

Day 1

Joshua 1:8
A Key to Success

Do not let this Book of the Law depart from your mouth; meditate on it day and night, so that you may be careful to do everything written in it. Then you will be prosperous and successful.

Does "depart from your mouth" mean "don't talk about it" or "don't stop talking about it"?

_____

_____

_____

_____

_____

_____

_____

_____

Day 2

Genesis 39:2
Success and God's Presence

The Lord was with Joseph and he prospered, and he lived in the house of his Egyptian master.

How would you say God is with you? Why?

_____

_____

_____

_____

_____

_____

_____

_____

Day 3

James 1:22
More Than Knowing

Do not merely listen to the word, and so deceive yourselves. Do what it says.

How is a fresh understanding of success affecting your life today?

_____

_____

_____

_____

_____

_____

_____

_____

_____

_____

_____

Day 4

Matthew 6:34
Living Today

Therefore do not worry about tomorrow, for tomorrow will worry about itself. Each day has enough trouble of its own.

In talking about worry, how was Jesus also talking about success?

_____

_____

_____

_____

_____

_____

_____

_____

_____

_____

_____

Day 5

Matthew 25:21
Succeeding with Who You Are

His master replied, "Well done, good and faithful servant! You have been faithful with a few things; I will put you in charge of many things. Come and share your master's happiness!"

What is standing between you and hearing Jesus say those words to you at the end of your life?

_____

_____

_____

_____

_____

_____

_____

_____

_____

_____

_____

Day 6

Summary
Use the following space to write any thoughts that God has put in your heart and mind about the things that we have looked at in this session and during your "Daily Reflections" time this week.

WEEKLY MEMORY VERSE

The Lord was with Joseph and he prospered, and he lived in the house of his Egyptian master.
Genesis 39:2

LISTEN

LEARN

LIVE

LOVING OTHERS

LOVING GOD

GOING DEEPER

SESSION 2

HAPPIN

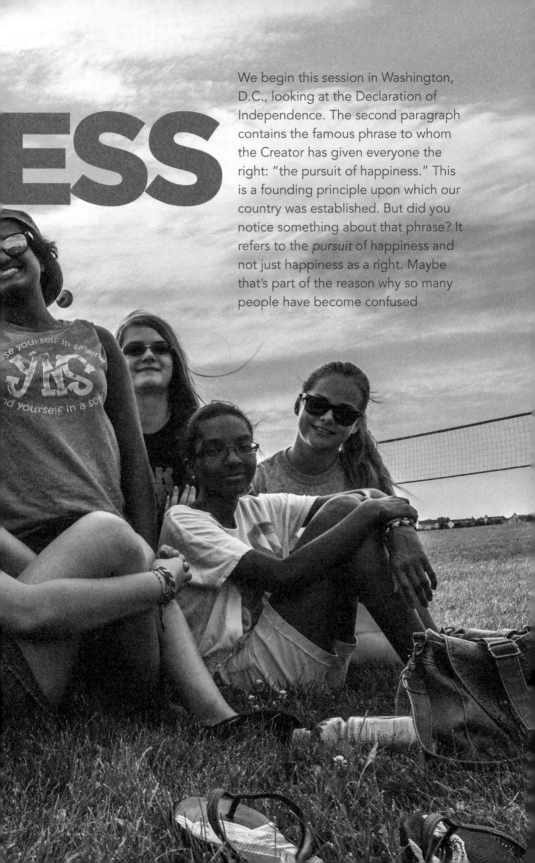

ESS

We begin this session in Washington, D.C., looking at the Declaration of Independence. The second paragraph contains the famous phrase to whom the Creator has given everyone the right: "the pursuit of happiness." This is a founding principle upon which our country was established. But did you notice something about that phrase? It refers to the *pursuit* of happiness and not just happiness as a right. Maybe that's part of the reason why so many people have become confused

about happiness. The founders didn't believe that we had a *right* to happiness; we have only a God-given right to pursue it!

The problem gets worse because most people also confuse happiness with feeling good or experiencing pleasure. When we aren't "happy" or are "unhappy," what we mean is that we either like and feel good about something or we don't like and feel good about something. In other words, we've limited happiness to an emotion—and a fickle one at that! After all, how many times have you felt unhappy and done something foolish or pursued happiness and found that it didn't really satisfy you?

In this second session, we will explore this widely used but often-misunderstood word, *happiness*. Then we will discover how God redefines happiness and shows us how to experience it and share it with others, especially to those who matter most.

LISTEN

Open your group with prayer. Focus on the lessons about words applied in the past week and invite group members to share their thoughts and insights about their own success during the past few days.

1. We are seeking to redefine happiness, but let's tip our hats to the Founding Fathers and talk a little bit about the word *pursuit*, as in *pursuit of happiness*. Describe one or two situations in your life where you would say that you *pursued* something or someone. What goes into an effective pursuit?

2. Most people want to live a healthy, balanced life. A regular medical check-up is a good way to measure health and spot potential problems. In the same way, a spiritual check-up is vital to your spiritual well being. The "Spiritual Health Assessment" was designed to give you a quick snapshot (or pulse) of your spiritual health. Take a few minutes alone to complete the "Spiritual Health Assessment" on page 135. After answering each question, tally your results. Then pair up with another person and briefly share one purpose that is going well and one that needs a little work.

LEARN

Most of us struggle with expectations of happiness and become frustrated in our pursuit. Too often we use the suggestions and guidelines that the world offers rather than listening to Jesus' instructions. Use the following questions to review and clarify the insights shared by Pastor Ross.

Watch the DVD teaching for this session now. We have provided space for you to take notes on page 48. There you can record any key thoughts, questions, and things that you want to remember or follow up on. After watching the video, have someone read the discussion questions in the "Learn" section and direct the discussion among the group. As you go through each of the subsequent sections, ask someone else to read the questions and direct the discussion.

3. What word does the Bible use to begin each of the Beatitudes in Matthew 5:3–11? How do the Beatitudes strike you when you read them with the word *happy* instead of *blessed*?

4. Pastor Ross suggests that one of the ways to finish Jesus' invitation, "Follow me," is to add "to happiness." What does that mean?

5. The first teaching point in the lesson explains that the real meaning of being blessed or happy is the result of having God's favor. This means that God is *for* you. For example, Romans 8:31–32 (italics added) says, "What, then, shall we say in response to these things? *If God is for us*, who can be against us? He who did not spare his own Son, but gave him up for us all—

mountain
Rugged style and frame for all road cycling

Schwinn
26" WOMEN'S RANGER BIKE

ROLL ME
to the
REGISTER
I'm ready
to go!

how will he not also, along with him, graciously give us all things?" Notice the italicized text? In what ways do you think God would "graciously give us happiness"?

6. Paul begins his letter to the Ephesians with this remarkable blessing: "Praise be to the God and Father of our Lord Jesus Christ, who has blessed us in the heavenly realms with every spiritual blessing in Christ" (Ephesians 1:3). What are some of the things that fit for you in the category of "*every* spiritual blessing"?

7. What does it mean to you to realize that happiness actually starts on the inside and is maintained by the degree to which we enjoy God and by what he gives us?

8. It turns out that the Founding Fathers were on to something. God urges us to pursue happiness by hungering and thirsting for righteousness (Matthew 5:6). How would you state Pastor Ross's explanation in your own words: "To hunger and thirst for righteousness is to desire to see right things prevail in the world"?

9. From our culture's point of view, happiness is a solitary pursuit, yet Christians are called into a body and given a place to bless and be blessed among other believers. How is life with other believers supposed to factor into our happiness?

LIVE

One of the marks of developing group intimacy is when we start disclosing things about ourselves that are not normal parts of conversation—like our failures. It is one thing to talk about societal, familial, or public figures' failures; it is something else entirely to come clean about our own. The way of happiness or joy includes self-disclosure, bearing one another's burdens, and just plain caring. Accountability with other Christians can be crucial to keeping us on track.

10. Pair up with someone in your group. (We suggest that men partner with men and women with women.) This person will be your *spiritual partner* for the rest of this study. He or she doesn't have to be your best friend but will simply encourage you to complete the goals that you set for yourself during this study. Following through on a resolution is tough when you're on your own, but we've found that it makes all the difference to have a partner who is cheering you on.

On pages 136–137 is a "Personal Health Plan," a chart for keeping track of your spiritual progress. Write your partner's name on page 137.

You have now begun to address two of God's four purposes for your life! They are part of the general way of happiness that God has designed for all of his children. You can see that the "Personal Health Plan" contains space for you to record the ups and downs of your progress each week in the column labeled "My Progress." With your spiritual partner, now you can do it together and not alone.

Tell your partner what step you chose. When you check in with your partner each week, the "Partner's Progress" column on this chart will provide a place to record your partner's progress in the goal that he or she chose.

11. Identify one or two experiences in your life that you would consider to be personal obstacles to happiness and ask your partner to help you re-examine what you might learn from those challenges. Seek to answer three questions:

Is there anything I can do to eliminate that obstacle?
Is it actually an obstacle, or am I still trying to find happiness under the world's standards?
What does this process tell me about my future happiness?

"We have limited

LOVING OTHERS

The Christian life always involves other people. The pursuit of happiness is not a straight line without detours. One of the aspects of real love for God and our neighbors is that small steps and mistakes matter. We stay engaged even when progress is slow. We care enough to correct, forgive, and seek forgiveness when mistakes occur. Those who do not love pretend not to care about their own happiness and do little to promote the joy of others.

But genuine relationships (reciprocal partnerships) deal with mistakes as minor steps in our journey toward God's best. They put us in the best place to learn from our failures. When we have someone commit to us for the long haul, we are more likely to face the possible shame and difficulty of having to set aside our pride and try another approach. Our ultimate happiness will include the failures and mistakes that we have overcome, as well as our progress in obedience to Christ.

12. How would you describe a relationship with Jesus Christ as the ultimate and perfect reciprocal partnership that promotes happiness? What did Jesus do for you to make that relationship a reality? How did he give and serve in such a way that he deserves to receive your ultimate trust (reference Ephesians 2:8–10)?

13. Take a look at the "Circles of Life" diagram on page 138 and write the names of two or three people you know who need to know Christ. Commit to praying for God's guidance and for an opportunity to share with each of them.

14. In what ways is talking with others about your relationship with Jesus an act of giving and serving? What might you receive as a result of your actions?

1appiness to an emotion."

LOVING GOD

God doesn't make mistakes. According to Ephesians 1:3, he has already structured everything in your life that you need for happiness. When it came to planning your destiny, no angels ever heard God mutter, "Oops!" He doesn't have to learn anything about us, yet it is amazing that he chooses to be in relationship with us people who are so prone to making mistakes on almost a daily basis. Much of our time in conversation with him ought to be spent seeking his direction and help regarding the lessons that we can learn from our mistakes. He is committed to producing a finished masterpiece of our lives. He is working for our true happiness and peace. As you go through the prayer exercises below, make sure that you are allowing the group to pray with you about things that you are trying to learn from God.

15. Share your prayer requests in your group and then gather in smaller circles of three or four people to pray. Be sure to have everyone write down the personal requests of the members to use as a reminder to pray for your group throughout the week. The "Prayer and Praise" section is on page 134.

Pray for one another in your circle. Do not put pressure on anyone to pray aloud. When you pray for each person, you may find it meaningful to hold hands or place your hands on another person's shoulder. Jesus often touched those whom he healed in order to communicate his care for them.

16. Take a few minutes to talk about what it would take to make time with God a priority every day or even five or six days a week. Do not demand an hour or even a half-hour of time; consider starting with a few minutes each day, and gradually you will desire more. Use the "Daily Reflections" at the end of each session for drawing near to God.

GOING DEEPER

Read the context for this session's memory verse: Ephesians 1:3–23. Paul starts with God's blessing and ends with a prayer that his readers will be able to see all that they have in Christ. Take some time to unpack these verses because they provide a foundation for happiness!

The act of blessing can be defined as "speaking or delivering good into someone's life." In what ways has Christ's presence in your life been the ultimate blessing?

What are some other spiritual blessings that God has delivered into your life?

Read the section between verses 3–14 in one take. Note the words that you may not understand, but try to summarize what Paul is telling the Ephesians. What's the main point?

Trace each of the times that *in Christ* or *through Christ* is used in verses 3–14. How is each significant?

Now read verses 15–23 without a pause. What are the highlights of Paul's prayer?

Summarize Christ's role in these verses. How does his position affect our hope of happiness now and for eternity?

REFLECTIONS

Day 1

Proverbs 15:13
It's on Your Face

A happy heart makes the face cheerful, but heartache crushes the spirit.

List and describe three specific actions or events that gladden your heart.

_____

_____

_____

_____

_____

_____

_____

_____

_____

_____

Day 2

Matthew 5:6
Healthy Hunger

Blessed are those who hunger and thirst for righteousness, for they will be filled.

How have you experienced the truth that a special kind of filling follows when a person does something good or righteous?

_____

_____

_____

_____

_____

_____

_____

_____

_____

_____

Day 3

Matthew 5:13
Happy Salt

"You are the salt of the earth. But if the salt loses its saltiness, how can it be made salty again? It is no longer good for anything, except to be thrown out and trampled underfoot."

Based on Jesus' words, what effect does the genuine joy of a Christian have on salting the world?

_____

_____

_____

_____

_____

_____

_____

_____

_____

_____

_____

_____

Day 4

Romans 8:31
God in Our Corner

What, then, shall we say in response to these things? If God is for us, who can be against us?

Is it better to read the "against us" as referring to opposition or referring to the fact that, no matter what the opposition, God is for us and will ensure a good result?

_____

_____

_____

_____

_____

_____

_____

_____

_____

_____

_____

_____

Day 5

Romans 8:28
God at Work

And we know that in all things God works for the good of those who love him, who have been called according to his purpose.

Why does this verse make you happy?

Day 6

Summary
Thinking about the things that we have looked at in this session and during your "Daily Reflections" time this week, use the following space to write any thoughts that God has put in your heart and mind.

WEEKLY MEMORY VERSE

Praise be to the God and Father of our Lord Jesus Christ, who has blessed us in the heavenly realms with every spiritual blessing in Christ.
Ephesians 1:3

_____

_____

_____

_____

_____

_____

_____

_____

_____

_____

_____

SESSION NOTES

LISTEN	LEARN	LIVE

LOVING OTHERS

LOVING GOD

GOING DEEPER

SESSION 3
HOLINE

SS

What do you think of when you hear the word *holiness*? It's probably not something warm and fuzzy. If you grew up outside church, then you probably think of holiness as "holier than thou" and remember church people being phony or, perhaps, "too good to be true." If you grew up in church, then you probably felt like holiness was something you didn't have and that God was mad at you because of it. If you're new to church, then you probably think that holiness is something you can never obtain. Why? Because holiness comes from the word *holy*, and being holy is either boring, impossible, or both.

The typical views of holiness, while common, miss what Jesus wants us to have and experience. Don't fall for the tricks of the devil or even society that implies that holiness is either impossible or for hypocrites. That's the wrong definition of holiness. It's a priceless word that begs for redefinition!

LISTEN

Open your group with prayer. Ask the group to share with one another the insights from the past two sessions that have made an impact on their lives. Practice a tone of thanksgiving in your prayer and affirm your realization that God isn't finished redefining your understanding of the Christian life.

Telling our personal stories builds deeper connections among group members. Choose one of the activities below to build your connections within the group.

1. Let's talk about experiences that you might have had with people who you thought were genuinely holy. Their lives were marked by a seemingly effortless and authentic presence of God, yet they were very real and in touch with life. What struck you most about them?

2. Sit with your spiritual partner. If your partner is absent, or if you are new to the group, join another pair or someone who doesn't yet have a partner. If you haven't established your spiritual partnership yet, do it now. (Refer to the session two "Live" section for help.)

Turn to the "Personal Health Plan" on page 137. Share with your partner how your time with God went this week. What is one thing you discovered? Did you make a commitment to a next step that you can share? What obstacles hindered you from following through this week? Make a note about your partner's progress and how you can pray for him or her.

3. Rotating leaders is one of the values that we highly recommend for your group. People need opportunities to experiment with ways in which God may have gifted them. Your group will give you all of the encouragement that you need before, during, and after the session.

We also suggest that you rotate host homes and have the host of each meeting provide the refreshments. Some groups like to let the host lead the meeting each week, while others like to let one person host while another person leads.

The "Small Group Calendar" on page 133 is a tool for planning who will host and lead each meeting. Take a few minutes to plan hosts and leaders for your remaining meetings. Do not pass this up! It will revolutionize your group.

Watch the DVD teaching for this session now. We have provided space for you to take notes on page 68. You can record any key thoughts, questions, and things that you want to remember or follow up on. After watching the video, have someone read the discussion questions in the "Learn" section and direct the discussion among the group. As you go through each of the subsequent sections, ask someone else to read the questions and direct the discussion.

LEARN

In this session, we are redefining and clarifying a familiar word that we hesitate to apply to ourselves. Hopefully the three points that Pastor Ross made about the meaning of the word helped to

give the word a fresh possibility for encouraging our relationship with God. Let's review the content of the lesson.

4. Pastor Ross opened his teaching with the point that many of us think of holiness as either a boring spirituality or an intimidating and unachievable perfection—or both! What

has been your impression of holiness?

5. The first characteristic of authentic holiness is belonging, as in "set apart" or "devoted." How would you explain the statement, "We are holy because we belong to God"?

6. Romans 12:1 says, "Therefore, I urge you, brothers, in view of God's mercy, to offer your bodies as living sacrifices, holy and pleasing to God—this is your spiritual act of worship." Would you say that this verse describes the act of becoming a Christian or the lifestyle of someone who is already a Christian? Why?

7. Pastor Ross's second point was that holiness also means *pursuing*. Why is it important to remember that being holy involves the fact of being set aside as well as the function of actively *becoming/pursuing* who we are? Include the following declaration in your discussion: "Jesus loves us as we are, but he doesn't leave us as he finds us!"

8. A third aspect of holiness that we heard about was *wholeness*. Two verses were used to explain how God is involved in our holiness or making us worthy

own

"Holy living changes the way we live with people."

to be called holy. How does each of these verses help you to understand holiness? "He restores my soul. He guides me in paths of righteousness for his name's sake" (Psalm 23:3). "Come to me, all you who are weary and burdened, and I will give you rest. Take my yoke upon you and learn from me, for I am gentle and humble in heart, and you will find rest for your souls" (Matthew 11:28–29).

LIVE

When we begin to get serious about holiness, the concept immediately affects every area of our lives. It's important to realize that another word that also translates from the original Greek word for *holiness* (hagiasmos) is the even more imposing word *sanctification*. Since we now have redefined holiness, sanctification isn't so intimidating. In fact, if we look at the word itself (sanct-ification), we discover that *sanctus* is simply another language's (Latin) version of *holy*. Holiness or sanctification is the immediate, ongoing goal when we understand that, as Pastor Ross put it, "The Christian life is more than just being forgiven; it also means to be different and to live differently." Holy is not only who we are; it's also the standard by which we seek to live—with God's help.

9. As he closed his remarks, Pastor Ross added a fourth characteristic of holiness—it's supernatural. Look again at Ephesians 1:14, which is part of the passage that we explored in the last session. How does the Holy Spirit help to resolve the issue that we cannot be godly or live holy lives on our own or in our own strength?

10. Practical holiness always boils down to obeying and stepping into opportunities that God places before us. Holiness has to do with finding what God has "set us apart" or "devoted us" to do in his kingdom. Is there an area of service that God has put on your heart to serve in your local church? How are you connecting that desire with your efforts to present your body as a living sacrifice? Commit to taking the first step and be willing to let God lead you to the ministry that expresses your passion for holiness. In your "Personal Health Plan" on page 136, answer the "Where are you serving?" question. If you are not currently serving, note one area in which you will consider serving.

LOVING OTHERS

The basics of holy living can be understood as applications of the central teachings of the Bible. For example, the Great Commandment is something that God wants every one of us to live in our lives. If we are not increasing our capacity and efforts at loving God and others, we fall short of holiness. Holy living affects not only our life *among* people; it also changes the way we live *with* people. God's real messengers communicate love even when the message is an unexpected one or a hard one.

11. In the last session, we asked you to write some names in the "Circles of Life" diagram. Who did you identify as the people in your life who need to meet Jesus? Go back to this diagram on page 138 to help you think of the various people with whom you come into contact on a regular basis and who need to know Jesus more deeply. Consider the following ideas for action and make a plan to follow through on one of them this week.

This is a wonderful time to welcome a few friends into your group. Which of the people whom you listed could you invite? It is possible that you may need to help your friend overcome real obstacles in order to come to a place where he or she can encounter Jesus? Does your friend need a ride to the group or help with childcare? Consider inviting a friend to attend a weekend service with you. You could even plan to enjoy a meal together afterward. This can be a great opportunity to talk with someone about your faith in Jesus.

Is there someone whom you would not invite to your group but who still needs a connection? Would you be willing to have lunch or coffee with that person, catch up on life, and share something you've learned from this study? Jesus doesn't call all of us to lead small groups, but he does call every disciple to spiritually multiply his or her life over time.

12. We are definitely not alone in being set apart or devoted to God. We are part of a larger plan. God has our lives in mind for something bigger than ourselves and bigger than what we can accomplish on our own. God's glory is worth whatever combination of good, bad, and bitter that he mixes for us because he intends to make his holy people more and more holy. How willing are you to surrender your plans and desires to God's plan for something bigger— something truly holy? What are your reservations?

The central point of holy living is the opportunity to love God. As the Great Commandment describes, our love for God takes everything we have. Loving God definitely includes listening *for* and listening *to* his messengers. It involves developing an attentive attitude about life and realizing that, at any time, on any day, God may find a way to get a word to us. God is working out our holiness every day. According to Ephesians 3:14–19, God's love is infinitely four-dimensional (breadth, length, height, and depth can't be measured), yet he offers it to us in Christ that we might love him in return. Loving God also involves trusting him with our needs and the needs of others.

13. Share your praises and prayer requests with one another. Record these on the "Prayer and Praise" section on page 134. Then spend time praying for each other.

14. End your meeting by singing a song together or closing the evening with a prayer.

GOING DEEPER

Everything we find in Scripture that relates to spiritual growth or to God's ongoing relationship with us has to do with holiness. If no other measurement was available, the long-suffering patience of God with his chosen (set apart) people would be a good enough reminder that he is in it with us for the long haul! Here are several passages that you may wish to explore as a group or on your own.

Read Ephesians 3:14–21, a passage we briefly mentioned in the lesson. This is one of Paul's great prayers for the Church—us. Note that it begins and ends with glory! As this amazing prayer is rolled out in our lives, God will be glorified (and we will be lifted and led to greater holiness).

How is this prayer a request for holiness?

When it comes to our shortcomings and sins, why is verse 20 a crucial fact to remember?

This prayer includes Father, Spirit, and Son. How does each one participate in Paul's vision of the Church?

What other personal encouragement do you draw from these verses?

"God is working

Read John 14:15–27.

During the Last Supper (John 13–17), Jesus devoted many of his remarks to the coming arrival of the Holy Spirit to energize, guide, and sustain the fledgling Church that would emerge from Jesus' resurrection. The Holy Spirit is the counselor whom Jesus promised would be active in the world and particularly among those set apart for Christ.

What will the Holy Spirit/ Counselor be sent by the Father to do?

Why is he called the Spirit of Truth?

According to verse 27, what will be the side effect of Jesus' gift of the Holy Spirit?

See John 16:5–15 for more on the Holy Spirit at work in the world.

out our holiness every day."

REFLECTIONS

Day 1

Psalm 23:3
Spiritual Restoration

"He restores my soul. He guides me in paths of righteousness for his name's sake."

How has soul restoration and ongoing guidance worked out in your walk with God?

_____

_____

_____

_____

_____

_____

_____

_____

_____

Day 2

II Corinthians 3:18
Going to Holiness

"And we, who with unveiled faces all reflect the Lord's glory, are being transformed into his likeness with ever-increasing glory, which comes from the Lord, who is the Spirit."

How does this passage help you to understand that holiness is an ongoing process that God is working out in your life?

_____

_____

_____

_____

_____

_____

_____

Day 3

Matthew 11:28–30

"Come to me, all you who are weary and burdened, and I will give you rest. Take my yoke upon you and learn from me, for I am gentle and humble in heart, and you will find rest for your souls. For my yoke is easy and my burden is light."

Why do you think the inclusion of rest in Christ is an important part of our redefinition of holiness? Where does the yoke fit?

Day 4

Ephesians 3:17b–19

"I pray that you, being rooted and established in love, may have power, together with all the saints [holy ones], to grasp how wide and long and high and deep is the love of Christ, and to know this love that surpasses knowledge—that you may be filled to the measure of all the fullness of God."

What would it take for you to be more "established" in love?

Day 5

I Corinthians 10:12
Humble Holiness

"So, if you think you are standing firm, be careful that you don't fall!"

What role does humility need to have in your pursuit of holiness?

Day 6

Summary
Use the following space to write any thoughts that God has put on your heart and mind about the things we have looked at in this session and during your "Daily Reflections" time this week.

_____

_____

_____

_____

_____

_____

_____

_____

_____

_____

WEEKLY MEMORY VERSE

Come to me, all you who are weary and burdened, and I will give you rest. Take my yoke upon you and learn from me, for I am gentle and humble in heart, and you will find rest for your souls. For my yoke is easy and my burden is light.
Matthew 11:28–30

LISTEN	LEARN	LIVE

LOVING OTHERS

LOVING GOD

GOING DEEPER

SESSION 4
GRACE

You've probably participated in word-association games. Here's one to try on people. Give them either word (*grace* or *amazing*), and they will likely come up with the other. People who don't even know what grace actually *is* have picked up the idea that, whatever it is, it's amazing!

One of the Christian heroes who emerged from World War II was a German pastor named Dietrich Bonhoeffer. In his book *The Cost of Discipleship*, he contrasted two understandings of grace: cheap and costly. Cheap grace is easy—it's easy to claim, easy to understand, easy to accept, and easy to take for granted. Costly grace is precious and becomes more precious the better we understand what our position would be if God had not decided to apply grace to us. Like all of the words that we've considered in this study, grace deserves another look, a redefinition for our time. Not a change of definition—that's already happened. We need to go back and understand grace as God (its source) intends for us to understand it.

LISTEN

Open your group with prayer. Thank God for the story that he is writing in the life of each person in your group. If possible, mention each of the group members by name in prayer. It is often surprising to discover people who have never heard their name mentioned out loud before God in prayer.

Telling personal stories builds deeper connections among group members. Choose one of the activities below to build your connections within the group.

1. Using an event or experience from your own life, how would you illustrate the significance or importance of grace?

2. Check in with your spiritual partner(s) or with another partner if yours is absent. Share something that God taught you during your time in his Word this week or read a brief section from your journal. Be sure to write down your partner's progress on page 137.

Watch the DVD teaching for this session now. We have provided space for you to take notes on page 88. There you can record any key thoughts, questions, and things that you want to remember or follow up on. After watching the video, have someone read the discussion questions in the "Learn" section and direct the discussion among the group members. As you go through each of the subsequent sections, ask someone else to read the questions and direct the discussion.

LEARN

The first thing we learned in this session's teaching is that grace is a concept, idea, or experience that sets Christianity apart from all other religions on earth. If we consider that religions can be described as various human efforts to reach or please God, it would stand to reason that a belief system originating with God, himself, would have a different flavor entirely. As Pastor Ross mentioned, when C.S. Lewis was asked what made Christianity unique from other religions, he did not hesitate in his reply: grace. Let's talk about it! Note that the following questions allow us to unpack the four points made about grace:

Grace is God's great favor.

Grace is God's beauty on us and in us.

Grace is God's gift offered to us.

Grace comes to us by faith.

3. Pastor Ross began by highlighting the meaning of grace as God's favor. How do you see or how have you experienced

God's overflowing abundance or expansive treatment of you?

4. What reasons would you give to make the case that the parable of the prodigal son might also be called the parable of the gracious father (see Luke 15:11–32)?

5. It's easy to claim that our encounters with God's grace change us. What examples illustrate Pastor Ross's point that grace actually transforms people in the direction of beauty?

6. Why do you think it's so hard for human beings to grasp the idea that grace is a gift? Ask someone to read Luke 7:36–50, then discuss all of the ways you find grace in that encounter between Jesus and people.

7. Pastor Ross mentioned that the more someone needs grace, the more grace God gives. Romans 5:20 says, "The law was added so that the trespass might increase. But where sin increased, grace increased all the more." Why is it important to remember that God's grace will never fall short of our needs?

8. The final teaching point created an opportunity for response. Pastor Ross mentioned Ephesians 2:8–9, which says, "For it is by grace you have been saved, through faith—and this not from yourselves, it is the gift of God—not by works, so that no one can boast." How do grace and faith work together so that God saves us?

"Costly grace

s precious."

"Grace sets

LIVE

One of the crucial statements of the Bible originates in Habakkuk 2:4 and is used in the New Testament (Romans 1:17, Galatians 3:11) to demonstrate that God has always had the same plan in dealing with his human creations: a relationship accessed by faith. "The righteous will live by his faith." This truth is illustrated by Abraham in the Old Testament when God notes, "Abram believed the Lord, and he credited it to him as righteousness" (Genesis 15:6). Paul uses Abraham in Galatians 3:6–14 to make the case that God's amazing grace has always been lived out by faith.

9. What are some places in your life in which you see God's grace most obviously in action? The Bible says that we "live by faith, not by sight" (II Corinthians 5:7), so what kind of "vision" is your faith allowing you to have of God's work in your life?

10. It's one thing to think about and talk about grace as an idea or subject. It's another thing to experience grace as the transforming power of God in your life. How would you describe your own access to God's grace through faith?

Christianity apart."

LOVING OTHERS

At one point in his teaching, Pastor Ross mentioned that grace offers us a new way to see God and all of life. We not only see and receive grace, but we are conduits of God's grace to others. People almost invariably point to both individuals and small groups as significant factors that God has used to express his grace. But these intersections are only as effective as we are willing to allow them to be in our lives. While we share in a small group, we are also surrounded by neighbors whom we are called by God to love as ourselves—to express the same grace that we have received.

Loving others can seem like a risk until we remember that, somewhere in life, those whom we have loved will probably have the chance to love us back when we least expect it. That is also one of the reasons why we have been so grateful that you have become part of a group. It is within community that you are able to find people who can lift your burdens, pray for you, and express genuine concern for you in your moments of crisis.

11. Take a few minutes to talk about ways that you may have experienced God's grace during your small group times.

12. Share with each other how you have done with inviting people on the "Circles of Life" to church or to your small group.

13. In your "Personal Health Plan" on page 136, answer the question, "Where are you serving and sharing your faith?"

LOVING GOD

As we begin to appreciate the abundant moments of grace in our lives and how God uses them, we can see that part of what it means to love God is to take God's reputation seriously. David summarized his day-to-day relationship with God in these familiar words: "He restores my soul; He guides me in the paths of righteousness for His name's sake" (Psalm 23:3). The phrase "for His name's sake" is about learning to love upholding God's reputation in our lives. The "paths of righteousness" are filled with God-arranged intersections! Both his restoration and his guidance in life are products of his grace.

Loving God means eagerly expanding our understanding of him, realizing that we will never come to the end of discovering more things about God. We have only scratched the surface of his grace.

14. Share your praises and prayer requests with one another. Record these on the "Prayer and Praise" section on page 134.

15. What specific "vacuums of grace" (places where grace is desperately needed) in your own life or in the lives of people around you are on your mind right now that the rest of the group can pray for this week? How can you claim Romans 5:20 in those situations?

GOING DEEPER

Pastor Ross used two of Jesus' parables in this session to illustrate aspects of grace. These stories are vivid reminders that grace shows up in the strangest places and is shamefully absent where it's needed most.

Read Luke 7:36–50.

Jesus is spending an evening with Simon the Pharisee and other guests. But Jesus gets special attention from a woman with a poor reputation. Simon knows her history and can hardly believe that Jesus would let the woman touch him. In Simon's eyes, that kind of unawareness of evil is a sure sign that Jesus isn't who he seems to be. Jesus corrects his perception with a story and a lesson.

How does Jesus contrast the actions of the woman with Simon's in the way that each treated Jesus?

In what ways did Jesus demolish Simon's observations rather than argue with them?

With whom do you identify most closely: the woman or Simon?

In what ways? Where could you do a better job in your treatment of Jesus?

Read Matthew 25:40 and discuss how it applies to this episode in Jesus' life and the episodes in your own lives.

Read Luke 15:11–32.

Luke 15 begins with a series of complaints against Jesus. He responds with three stories to address the issue of why he spent time with sinners. The third

story is the famous parable of the prodigal son. Jesus presents a case study of a father and two sons, one of whom leaves home with his inheritance and wastes it in sinful living. The climax of the story is the wandering son's return and the reception that he receives from his father.

What kinds of people would you say that each of the sons represents?

Which one most represents you? In what ways does the father in this story demonstrate grace?

Why can't the older brother show grace to his little brother? Does his struggle parallel relationships in your own life? How?

What can we learn from the parable of the prodigal son?

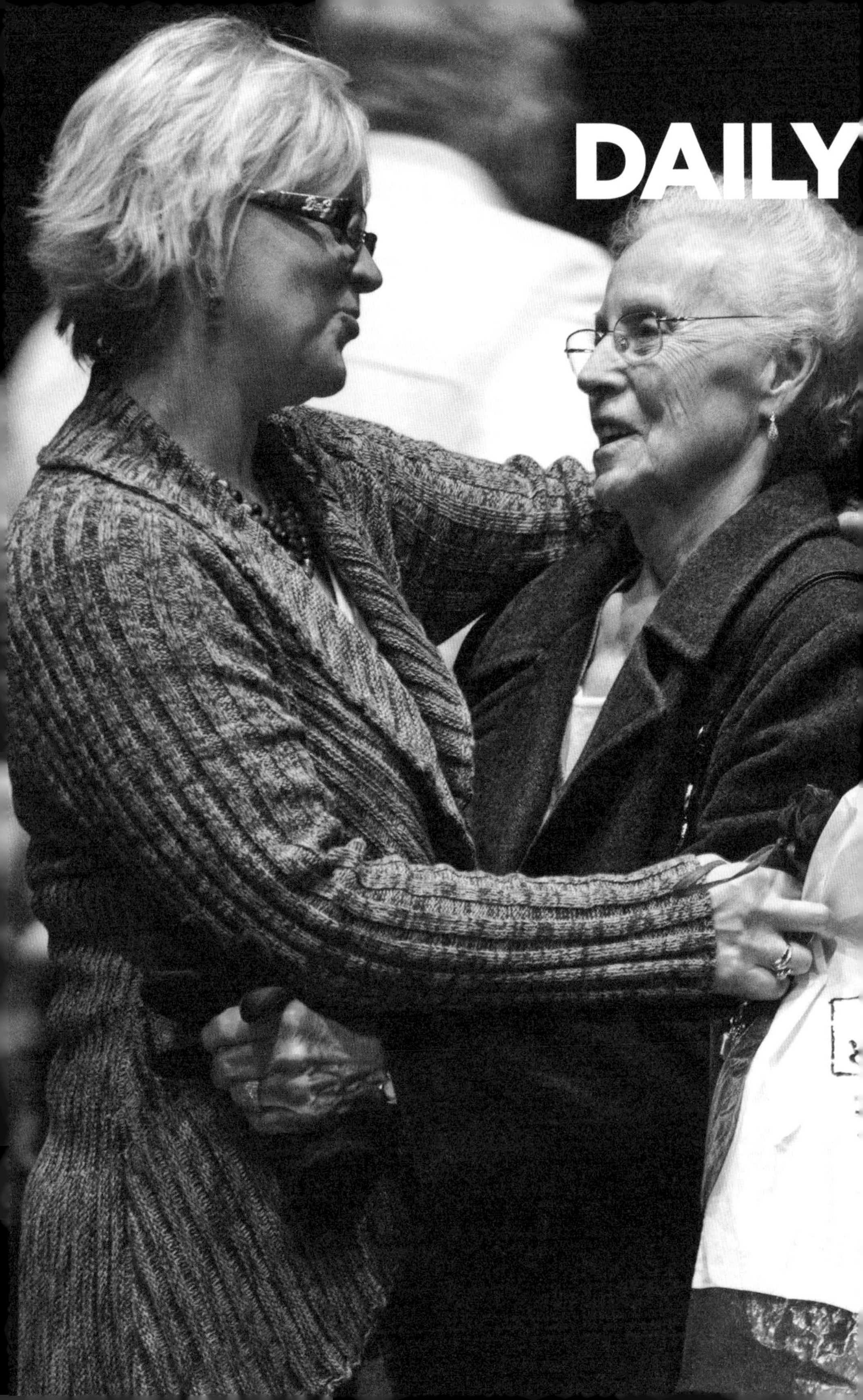

DAILY

REFLECTIONS

Day 1

Ephesians 2:8–9
Receiving the Gift

"For it is by grace you have been saved, through faith—and this not from yourselves, it is the gift of God—not by works, so that no one can boast."

How do these two verses include all four points made about grace in this week's session: favor, beauty, gift, and by faith?

_____

_____

_____

_____

_____

_____

_____

_____

Day 2

Matthew 13:44
Stumbling on Grace

"The kingdom of heaven is like a treasure hidden in the field, which a man found and hid again; and from joy over it he goes and sells all that he has and buys that field."

How does this very short parable by Jesus point to the most important intersection in any person's life?

_____

_____

_____

_____

_____

_____

_____

_____

Day 3

Luke 7:47
Motivated by Grace

"Therefore, I tell you, her many sins have been forgiven—for she loved much. But he who has been forgiven little loves little."

Was Jesus telling Simon he didn't have much that needed forgiveness, or was he showing Simon he hadn't received much of the forgiveness that he badly needed?

_____

_____

_____

_____

_____

_____

_____

_____

_____

_____

_____

Day 4

Habakkuk 2:4
Living by Faith

"See, he is puffed up; his desires are not upright—but the righteous will live by his faith."

Does living by faith lead to righteousness, or does one need to be righteous to live by faith? Why?

_____

_____

_____

_____

_____

_____

_____

_____

_____

_____

_____

Day 5

Titus 3:4–7
How God Did It

"But when the kindness and love of God our Savior appeared, he saved us, not because of righteous things we had done, but because of his mercy. He saved us through the washing of rebirth and renewal by the Holy Spirit, whom he poured out on us generously through Jesus Christ our Savior, so that, having been justified by his grace, we might become heirs having the hope of eternal life."

Grace is mentioned once, but where else do you see it in these verses? How much is up to God, and how much is up to us?

_____

_____

_____

_____

_____

_____

_____

Day 6

Summary
Use the following space to write any thoughts that God has put in your heart and mind about the things that we have looked at in this session and during your "Daily Reflections" time this week.

WEEKLY MEMORY VERSE

For it is by grace you have been saved, through faith—and this not from yourselves, it is the gift of God—not by works, so that no one can boast.
Ephesians 2:8–9

LISTEN

LEARN

LIVE

LOVING OTHERS

LOVING GOD

GOING DEEPER

SESSION 5
STEWAR

word *stewardship*. This word (at least in church circles) has become somewhat synonymous with giving money. Maybe that's why so many people cringe or roll their eyes and think, "Here the preacher goes again—always wanting more of my money." Well, hold on. Don't be so quick to jump to conclusions. Yes, the word *stewardship* is often used to emphasize generosity, but did you know that giving money is only a small aspect of what this word means? In fact, in the secular world, the concept of stewardship as a type of religious fundraising is hard to find.

From Webster to Wikipedia, the definition of the word *stewardship* means, first and foremost, the idea of "an ethic that embodies the responsible planning and management of resources." Stewardship is better seen as being applied to the environment, economics, health, property, and

DSHIP

information—not just religion. Many experts even link stewardship to the principles of sustainability.

In this study, we are redefining. We are going back to original definitions, or, more importantly, we are going to recapture the definition that God gave us in the first place. As we have seen so clearly over these past few weeks, when we use words as God defines them, we always gain a fresh and life-changing view of a word. We will now discover the same truth about stewardship.

LISTEN

Open your group with prayer. Ask for volunteers to pray, expressing to God what they have learned to this point in your group sessions. Telling personal stories builds deeper connections among group members. Choose one of the activities below to build your connections within the group.

1. Ask someone to read aloud the introduction paragraphs above for the group. Given the challenge to expand our understanding of the word *stewardship*, how would you describe your current understanding of the word? If the people who know you best were asked to come up with a list of ten words that most reminded them of you, would *steward* be on that list? Why or why not?

2. Check with your spiritual partner or with another partner if yours is absent. Talk about any challenges that you are currently facing in reaching the goals that you have set throughout this study. Tell your spiritual partner how he or she has helped you to follow through with each step. Be sure to write down your partner's progress on page 137.

3. Our next session is the last in this study. In the "Loving God" section of session six on page 118,

LEARN

Several times in these sessions, Pastor Ross has mentioned the famous philosopher Fezzig, the giant from the movie *The Princess Bride*. His pithy observation, "I do not think that word means what you think it means," has become the starting point for us in each of these studies. We're looking at words that we may have used often without really thinking about their meaning or whether the meaning that we were assigning to them was correct. This is allowing us to redefine words so that they, again, become the powerful guides that they were originally intended to be. Let's look at the three points of redefinition that Pastor Ross makes about the word *stewardship*.

you will have an opportunity to share "The Lord's Supper." Read the instructions and talk about your plans to prepare for that powerful, time-honored experience before you leave today.

Watch the DVD teaching for this session now. We have provided space for you to take notes on page 106. There you can record any key thoughts, questions, and things that you want to remember or follow up on. After watching the video, have someone read the discussion questions in the "Learn" section and direct the discussion among the group. As you go through each of the subsequent sections, ask someone else to read the questions and direct the discussion.

4. As a synonym for stewardship, Pastor Ross suggested the word *responsibility*. Paul wrote in I Corinthians 4:2, "Now it is required that those who have been given a trust must prove faithful." The phrase "those who have been given a trust" translates from the Greek word *oikonomous*, which is usually translated into the word *stewards*. Interestingly enough, we also get the word *economy*.

Steward is actually a description of a role/responsibility. What would be the difference between a good and a bad steward?

5. Our definition of biblical stewardship: recognizing that everything belongs to God. Whether over much or little, everything we are or have is a sacred trust or responsibility. What happens if we forget or reject this picture of stewardship?

6. Pastor Ross mentioned the commendation received by the effective servant in Matthew 24:45: "Who then is the faithful and wise servant, whom the master has put in charge of the servants in his household to give them their food at the proper time?" How can this statement encourage someone to live responsibly?

7. How do you understand the aspect of honor that is an important part of faithful stewardship as Pastor Ross explained from the parable of the wicked tenants in Matthew 21:33–41? (See, in particular, verse 39 where the word *honor* is sometimes translated into *respect*.)

8. Look at the verse quoted in question six. We often hear these words used in describing God's final account of our lives. But the setting in the parable (and in our lives) is often a partial or temporary account of life-to-a-point. Pastor Ross made his third point about stewardship: the fact that God will trust us with more if we will prove faithful with what he has already given. What examples can you think of from your life or someone else's life where increased responsibility/stewardship was given because of faithfulness in smaller areas?

"Biblical stewardship

LIVE

As this series begins to conclude, take stock of where you are. Before you focus on where God might take you, think about how he brought you to this particular place. Every word that we have examined in this study, even with a new definition, remains simply a word unless it affects the way we actually live. The process of ongoing change may start with taking some time to recognize how God has been working and speaking into your life through this small group.

9. Take a few minutes to discuss the future of your group. How many of you are willing to stay together as a group and work through another study? If you have time, turn to the "Small Group Agreement" on page 132 and talk about any changes that you would like to make as you move forward as a group.

10. As you survey your current life surroundings, what areas or life skills do you think would be helpful for your group to work on together in the weeks and months to come? How are you practicing stewardship of your abilities and resources in this group?

11. A year from now, in what ways would you like to be in a different situation? In what ways would you like to be a different you?

ecognizing that everything belongs to God."

LOVING OTHERS

Even in a fairly small group, expect to notice a significant sample of various stages of success and setbacks in stewardship awareness and participation. Some will be "there," while others are on the way in or on the way out. The strength of a small group can be seen in the capacity of people "at different places" to pray for, to care for, and to encourage people who are at different places in God's plan for them. We can laugh with those who laugh and weep with those who weep.

12. Take some time to let people share where they see themselves on the continuum of God revealing their particular stewardship responsibilities and challenges. Pray for each other regarding the best way to relate to one another, to situations, and to God while in our particular places in life. Take some time also to talk a little about how the lessons in this series have affected your relationships outside the group.

LOVING GOD

According to the Great Commandment, loving God takes everything we have: heart, soul, mind, and strength. Loving God means accepting his promise of a plan for our future, even when we cannot see it. It means continuing to trust in the dark what we knew was true in the light. Our persistence in worship and continual efforts to improve our hunger for God are steps toward a clearer sense of stewardship.

13. Turn to the "Personal Health Plan" on page 136 and individually consider the question, "How are you surrendering your heart?" Share some of your thoughts in the group.

14. Share your praises and prayer requests with one another. Record these on the "Prayer and Praise" section on page 134. Then pray together for each other.

GOING DEEPER

Read Matthew 24: 36–51. Jesus is speaking about conditions leading to the final moment of history, but the terms can be applied to the culminating moments of anyone's life. We all live a breath away from eternity. Will the Lord find us doing what we are supposed to be doing when he comes for us or when we go to him?

How does this passage actually describe almost any life at any time before death or before Christ comes?

What does it mean to "keep watch"?

Describe the duties/ responsibilities of the steward that Jesus was talking about.

In looking at the stewards' actions (both good and bad), what areas are personal or private, and what areas involve other people?

In what specific areas do your own stewardship responsibilities extend to others beyond yourself? How is your current faithfulness record?

DAILY

REFLECTIONS

Day 1

II Chronicles 16:9
God's Quest

"For the eyes of the Lord range throughout the earth to strengthen those whose hearts are fully committed to him. You have done a foolish thing, and from now on you will be at war."

Think today about your heart toward God. To what degree would he find it "fully committed to him" when he reviews your life?

_____

_____

_____

_____

_____

_____

Day 2

Proverbs 3:5–6
Who Is the Master?

"Trust in the Lord with all your heart and do not lean on your own understanding. In all your ways acknowledge Him, and He will make your paths straight."

Stewardship doesn't happen in a vacuum. Regular acknowledgment of the Master is significant. How are you reporting regularly to the Lord about your own life of stewardship?

_____

_____

_____

_____

_____

_____

Day 3

Matthew 6:33–34
Kingdom Stewards

"But seek first His kingdom and His righteousness, and all these things will be added to you. So do not worry about tomorrow; for tomorrow will care for itself. Each day has enough trouble of its own."

In what ways does your personal stewardship pattern fit the picture of seeking first the Master's kingdom and his righteousness?

Day 4

I Corinthians 4:2
Expected Faithfulness

"Now it is required that those who have been given a trust must prove faithful."

We haven't redefined the word *faithful* in our study, but how are you currently using it in your relationship with God?

Day 5

Luke 17:10
Humble Stewardship

"So you also, when you have done everything you were told to do, should say, 'We are unworthy servants; we have only done our duty.'"

You may find it helpful to back up and read Luke 17:1–9. How are you allowing your understanding of grace to affect your practices of stewardship?

_____

_____

_____

_____

_____

_____

_____

_____

_____

_____

Day 6

Summary
Use the following space to write any thoughts that God has put in your heart and mind about the things that we have looked at in this session and during your "Daily Reflections" time this week.

WEEKLY MEMORY VERSE

Who then is the faithful and wise servant, whom the master has put in charge of the servants in his household to give them their food at the proper time? It will be good for that servant whose master finds him doing so when he returns.
Matthew 24:45–46

LISTEN

LEARN

LIVE

LOVING OTHERS

LOVING GOD

GOING DEEPER

LOVE

Can you think of a more significant word to wrap up our video series than *love*? The word *love* means as many different things to as many different people as any word out there. It may even be the most misunderstood word in the entire English language. We say that we love ice cream and love the summers in Chicago. We even love the Cubs (sometimes). We love 40% off sales, and we love a day off (that's

for sure). Sometimes we actually love friends and family, too. We fall in love, and we fall out of love (which sounds a lot like some kind of cosmic accident, doesn't it?). All too often, we even confuse love with sexual attraction. What love ought to mean should go way beyond what we like or enjoy. To love someone means to care deeply about them to the point of making a firm commitment to them. Sure, pleasure and joy should be part of the equation, but, without commitment, love is only a feeling, and feelings are not strong enough to help you through the hard times.

Bottom line, how often do we stop and think about what God's definition of love is? When we do, what we discover forces us to redefine the way we use that word.

LISTEN

Open your group with prayer. Thank God for the experiences of the last five weeks and ask for his wisdom in this final session and for deciding on a plan for the future of the group.

1. If your group is active and playful, highlight each person for a few moments and have the rest of the group offer suggestions about their positive character traits and what they bring to the group.

2. God has our future in his hands and knows it already, but he will not reveal it all to us until the time is right for each development. How does that make you feel?

3. Take time in this final session to connect with your spiritual partner. What has God been showing you about yourself through these sessions? Check in with each other about the progress that you have made in your spiritual growth during this study. Make plans about whether you will continue your relationship with your spiritual partner outside your Bible study group.

Watch the DVD teaching for this session now. We have provided space for you to take notes on page 126. There you can record any key thoughts, questions, and things that you want to remember or follow up on. After watching the video, have someone read the discussion questions in the "Learn" section and direct the discussion among the group. As you go through each of the subsequent sections, ask someone else to read the questions and direct the discussion.

LEARN

Most of us would have probably guessed that we would see the word *love* on the *Redefine* list sooner or later. While introducing this session, Pastor Ross noted that aspects from all of the other words that we have redefined in this study have some light to shed on love. Whatever frustrations and heartache we may feel about the word, the complex experiences that it describes remain as central longings in our lives. We were created to need and express love in our relationships with others. Let's review and expand the teaching that we just heard.

4. Isn't it interesting that God took a little-used word for love in Greek, *agape*, and made it the term that describes what he gives and who he is? I John 4:8 says, "Whoever does not love does not know God, for God is love." Both times that the word *love* is used in that verse, it's *agape*. What does this verse mean?

5. The first concept that Pastor Ross connected with agape love is "incomprehensible value." What impact does it have on a person to know that they are more than they can imagine to someone else—in this case, to God?

6. Right after pricelessness came "unfathomable meaning" as a part of what is communicated by agape love. According to John 3:16, God not only put a down

payment on us, but he also made a payment-in-full for us because, as Pastor Ross put it, "I love what you can become." How does bottomless or endless meaning affect your understanding of the nature of God's love?

7. The third concept that clarifies agape love is "undeserved commitment." John 13:1 says, "It was just before the Passover Feast. Jesus knew that the time had come for him to leave this world and go to the Father. Having loved his own who were in the world, he now showed them the full extent of his love." Jesus would be dead in less than twenty-four hours, and he knew it. What practical action did he take in those intense moments of realizing how close death and suffering were (see John 13:1–17)? How was that underserved commitment?

8. A key verse that illustrates all of agape love but highlights the fourth aspect is John 3:16: "For God so loved the world that he gave his one and only Son, that whoever believes in him shall not perish but have eternal life." How does this verse convey the sacrificial nature of agape love?

9. The fifth aspect of agape love that Pastor Ross mentioned was the supernatural nature of love. We can't generate it, so where does it come from? Look up I John 4:19 and answer the question, knowing that both times that the word *love* is used, it translates into *agape*. Why does this verse matter when we are thinking about the importance of loving others?

 Hopefully our times together have been a real encouragement as we have sought to experience all that God has to offer when we realize the words that have become stale or misused. These words have been redefined to express in powerful ways the message of the Gospel and the ways that God wants to work in and through our lives.

10. How would you describe the impact of these Bible lessons on your thought patterns and the language you use to talk with others about your relationship with God?

11. If your group still needs to make decisions about continuing to meet after this session, have that discussion now. Talk about what you will study, who will lead it, and where and when you will meet.

Review your "Small Group Agreement" on page 132 and evaluate how well you met your goals. Discuss any changes that you want to make as you move forward. As your group starts a new study, this is a great time to take on a new role or change roles of service in your group. What new role will you take on? If you are uncertain, maybe your group members have some ideas for you. Remember, you are not making a life-long commitment to this new role; it will only be for a few weeks. Maybe someone would like to share a role with you if you do not feel ready to serve solo.

LOVING OTHERS

Very few Christians can honestly claim to be solitary successes in spiritual growth or have self-instructed expansion of understanding of the things of God. Obviously, we do not even become Christians without God's direct, gracious intervention on our behalf. There are no self-made believers. The impact of a small group experience, if we allow it, reminds us that we share a lot in common with other people and that we can often gain significant insight into what God is doing in our lives when we love others enough to observe what he is doing in their lives! Using our redefined words with each other and lovingly correcting one another will go a long way as we strive to become the kind of people whom God wants to use as salt and light in the world.

12. From the past five weeks (involving a fresh understanding of success, happiness, holiness, grace, stewardship, and love), what examples can you think of that you learned from and responded differently to in the company of this group?

13. Based on everything that you have thought about in these sessions, what would you say it means to thrive in the Christian life in God-pleasing and God-defined ways?

LOVING GOD

Even though we often think of loving God as an individual response, expressing that love and experiencing his immediate response actually occurs regularly in the company of other Christians. Do not overlook the following opportunity to practice a powerful, time-honored way for believers to tangibly express their love for God and for one another. There are reasons why most of these actions involve grace. Among the most powerful is sharing in the Lord's Supper (also called Communion) with each other. Instructions for how to share in this powerful experience are included in this workbook.

14. If you have chosen to share the Lord's Supper, you may do that now. Instructions are found on pages 139–140.

15. Close by praying for your prayer requests and take a couple of minutes to review the praises that you have recorded over the past five weeks on the "Prayer and Praise" section on page 134. Thank God for what he has done in your group during this study.

GOING DEEPER

Read Mark 12:28-34.

In this conversation a day or two before Jesus' trip to the cross, Jesus was asked an honest question. Someone wanted to know what was the "bottom line," the "main thing," and the most important commandment. Jesus answered him immediately, and he completely agreed with Jesus' answer!

Heart, soul, mind, strength. Come up with at least one example of loving God using each of these terms.

How significant is it that Jesus and the scribe agreed about the answer?

Why did Jesus tell him, "You are not far from the kingdom of heaven"?

Read John 13:1-17.

Jesus already feels the weight of the cross, but he loves his disciples more. He not only takes the time to have a last Passover with them and speak to them about many significant matters that they will need to know later, but he also gives them a visual and felt lesson that they will never forget. What do you think John meant by "he now showed them the full extent of his love"?

How do we know from this little episode that Jesus was aware of the big picture and that he knew what was about to happen?

How was doing the unexpected an amazing act of love?

Foot washing was primarily practical and necessary at the time, not symbolic. What kinds of selfless acts today might parallel what Jesus did for his disciples?

How did Jesus, himself, apply what he had done?

REFLECTIONS

Day 1

John 3:16
Love Like No Other

"For God so loved the world that he gave his one and only Son, that whoever believes in him shall not perish but have eternal life."

How have you received the invitation found in this verse?

_____

_____

_____

_____

_____

_____

_____

_____

Day 2

I Corinthians 13:4-7
Love's Qualities

"Love is patient, love is kind. It does not envy, it does not boast, it is not proud. It is not rude, it is not self-seeking, it is not easily angered, it keeps no record of wrongs. Love does not delight in evil but rejoices with the truth. It always protects, always trusts, always hopes, always perseveres."

What qualities of love do you need to ask God to build into your life more?

_____

_____

_____

_____

_____

_____

Day 3

I John 2:4–5
Where Love Lives

"The man who says, 'I know him,' but does not do what he commands is a liar, and the truth is not in him. But if anyone obeys his word, God's love is truly made complete in him."

When did your growing love for God lead to greater obedience?

_____

_____

_____

_____

_____

_____

_____

_____

_____

_____

_____

Day 4

Romans 8:38–39
Inseparable Love

"For I am convinced that neither death nor life, neither angels nor demons, neither the present nor the future, nor any powers, neither height nor depth, nor anything else in all creation, will be able to separate us from the love of God that is in Christ Jesus our Lord."

Why exactly are you glad today that nothing can separate you from the love of God in Christ?

_____

_____

_____

_____

_____

_____

_____

_____

_____

Day 5

John 21:17
Loving Persistence

"The third time he said to him, 'Simon son of John, do you love me?' Peter was hurt because Jesus asked him the third time, 'Do you love me?' He said, 'Lord, you know all things; you know that I love you.' Jesus said, 'Feed my sheep.'"

How often does Jesus have to gently instruct you before you really listen? Why do you think he doesn't give up?

_____

_____

_____

_____

_____

_____

_____

_____

_____

_____

Day 6

Summary
Use the following space to write any thoughts that God has put in your heart and mind about the things that we have looked at in this session and during your "Daily Reflections" time this week.

WEEKLY MEMORY VERSE

For God so loved the world that he gave his one and only Son, that whoever believes in him shall not perish but have eternal life.
John 3:16

LISTEN	LEARN	LIVE

LOVING OTHERS	LOVING GOD	GOING DEEPER

APPE

FREQUENTLY ASKED QUESTIONS

What do we do on the first night of our group?

Like all fun things in life, have a party! A "get to know you" coffee, dinner, or dessert is a great way to launch a new study. You may want to review the "Small Group Agreement" on page 132 and share the names of a few friends whom you can invite to join you. But, most importantly, have fun before your study time begins.

Where do we find new members for our group?

This can be troubling, especially for new groups that have only a few people or for existing groups that lose a few people along the way. We encourage you to pray with your group and then brainstorm a list of people from work, church, your neighborhood, your children's school, family, the gym, and so forth. Then have each group member invite several people on his or her list.

No matter how you find members, it's vital that you stay on the lookout for new people to join your group. All groups tend to go through healthy attrition—the result of moves, releasing new leaders, ministry opportunities, and so forth. If the group gets too small, it could be at risk of shutting down. If you and your group stay open, you'll be amazed at the people God sends your way. The next person just might become a friend for life. You never know!

How long will this group meet?

It's totally up to the group once you come to the end of this six-week study. Most groups meet weekly for at least their first six weeks, but every other week can work, as well. We strongly recommend that the group meet for the first six weeks on a weekly basis if at all possible. This allows for continuity, and if people miss a meeting, they aren't gone for a whole month.

At the end of this study, each group member may decide if he or she wants to continue for another six-week study. Some groups launch relationships for years to come, and others are stepping-stones into another group experience. Either way, enjoy the journey.

Can we do this study on our own?

Absolutely! This may sound crazy, but one of the best ways to do this study is not with a full house but with a few friends. You may choose to gather with one other couple with whom you would enjoy going to the movies or having a quiet dinner and then walking through this study. Jesus will be with you even if there are only two of you (Matthew 18:20).

What if this group is not working for us?

You're not alone! This could be the result of a personality conflict, life-stage difference, geographical distance, level of spiritual maturity, or any number of things. Relax. Pray for God's direction, and at the end of this six-week study, decide whether to continue with this group or find another. You don't buy the first car you look at or marry the first person you date, and the same goes for a group. Don't bail out before the six weeks are up; God might have something to teach you. Also, don't run from conflict or prejudge people before you give them a chance. God is still working in you, too!

Who is the leader?

Most groups have an official leader. Ideally, the group will mature, and members will rotate the leadership of meetings. We have discovered that healthy groups rotate hosts/leaders and homes on a regular basis. This model ensures that all members grow, give their unique contribution, and develop their gifts. This study guide and the Holy Spirit can keep things on track even when you rotate leaders. Christ has promised to be in your midst as you gather. Ultimately, God is your leader each step of the way.

How do we handle the childcare needs in our group?

Very carefully. Seriously, this can be a sensitive issue. We suggest that you empower the group to openly brainstorm solutions. You may try one option that works for a while and then adjust over time. Our favorite approach is for adults to meet in the living room or dining room and to share the cost of a babysitter (or two) who can be with the kids in a different part of the house. This way, parents don't have to be away from their children all evening when their children are too young to be left at home. A second option is to use one house for the kids and a second house (close by or a phonecall away) for the adults. A third idea is to rotate the responsibility of providing a lesson or care for the children either in the same house or in another house nearby. This can be an incredible blessing for kids. Finally, the most common idea is to decide that you need to have a night to invest in your spiritual lives individually or as a couple and to make your own arrangements for childcare. No matter what decision the group makes, the best approach is to dialogue openly about both the problem and the solution.

SMALL GROUP AGREEMENT

Group Attendance	To give priority to the group meeting. We will call or email if we will be late or absent. (Completing the Group Calendar will minimize this issue.)
Safe Environment	To help create a safe place where people can be heard and feel loved. (Please, no quick answers, snap judgments, or simple fixes.)
Respect Differences	To be gentle and gracious to people with different spiritual maturity, personal opinions, temperaments, or "imperfections" in fellow group members. We are all works in progress.
Confidentiality	To keep anything that is shared strictly confidential and within the group, and to avoid sharing improper information about those outside the group.
Encouragement for Growth	To be not just takers but givers of life. We want to spiritually multiply our lives by serving others with our God-given gifts.
Shared Ownership	To remember that every member is a minister and to ensure that each attender will share a small team role or responsibility over time.
Rotating Hosts/ Leaders and Homes	To encourage different people to host the group in their homes, and to rotate the responsibility of facilitating each meeting. (See the Group Calendar)

Our Times Together:

- Refreshments/mealtimes _____
- Childcare _____
- When we will meet (day of week) _____
- Where we will meet (place) _____
- We will begin at (time) _____ and end at _____
- We will do our best to have some or all of us attend a worship service together.
  Our primary worship service time will be _____
- Date of this agreement _____
- Date we will review this agreement again _____
- Who (other than the leader) will review this agreement at the end of this study
  _____

SMALL GROUP CALENDAR

Date	Lesson	Host Home	Refreshments	Leader
11/16	1	Steve and Laura's	Joe	Bill

PRAYER AND PRAISE

	Prayer Requests	Praise Reports
Session 1	Lindsey - Glucose pregnancy test + Sidney - Daughters homecoming bun & safe Tony - Bre's pregnancy Bre - concern for her mother/peace Me - Appreciating my time w/ family here	
Session 2	Tony - Bring back the focus to God Bre - Dad's visit Lindsey - Me - Dad's visit Allison -	
Session 3		
Session 4		
Session 5		
Session 6		

SPIRITUAL HEALTH ASSESSMENT

Just Beginning = 1   Getting Going = 3   Well Developed = 5

WORSHIP

I am experiencing more of the presence and power of God in my everyday life.   (1) 2 3 4 5

I am faithfully attending the weekend services and my small group to worship God.   (1) 2 3 4 5

I understand and practice biblical principles of stewardship in each of the major arenas of my life, particularly in my personal spending and giving.   (1) 2 3 4 5

I am seeking to please God by surrendering every area of my life to him (health, decisions, finances, relationships, future, etc.).   (1) 2 3 4 5

TOTAL

GROW

I am involved in an ongoing group/class study of God's Word.   1 (2) 3 4 5

I regularly discover spiritual insights and truths in my personal study of the Bible.   (1) 2 3 4 5

I am experiencing more of the characteristics of Jesus Christ (love, joy, peace, patience, kindness, self-control) in my life than a year ago.   1 2 (3) 4 5

I am able to explain the basic truths of the Christian faith to others.   1 2 (3) 4 5

TOTAL

CONNECT

I am deepening my understanding of and friendship with God in community with others.   1 2 (3) 4 5

I am growing in my ability to share and show my love to others.   1 2 (3) 4 5

I am committed to honest self-disclosure and can open up to a trusted friend about my struggles.   1 2 3 4 (5)

I agree with the ministry, vision and values of my church and am willing to partner with this local body of believers in Christ.   1 2 3 4 (5)

TOTAL

SERVE

I have discovered and am further developing my unique God-given gifts for ministry.   (1) 2 3 4 5

I can see how my gifts fit with others at church.   (1) 2 3 4 5

I am serving in a regular ministry (once a month or more) in the church or community.   (1) 2 3 4 5

I am regularly sharing my faith with friends and family, as well as at work and through neighborhood involvement.   (1) 2 3 4 5

TOTAL

PERSONAL HEALTH PLAN

This worksheet could become your single most important feature in this study. On it, you can record your personal priorities before the Father. It will help you to live a healthy spiritual life that balances all four of God's purposes.

PURPOSE	PLAN
WORSHIP	How are you surrendering your heart? Attend services more regularly Find an outlet for giving (volunteer) Devotional book Participate more w/ singing
CONNECT	Who are you connecting with spiritually? Small group, family
GROW	What is your next step for growth? Continuing to be active in the group and services ~~Participating more the~~
SERVE	Where are you serving and sharing your faith? Would like to serve w/ volunteer - Currently contributing to the group

Spiritual Partner's Name:

DATE	MY PROGRESS	PARTNER'S PROGRESS

CIRCLES OF LIFE

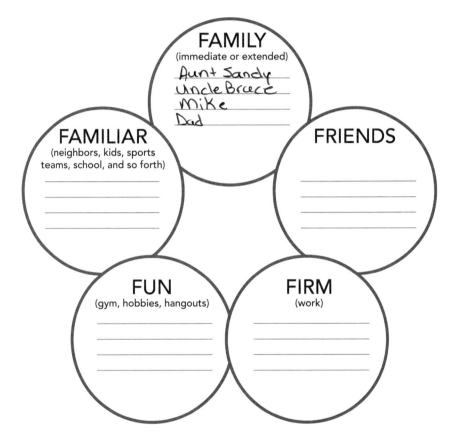

FAMILY
(immediate or extended)

Aunt Sandy
Uncle Bruce
Mike
Dad

FAMILIAR
(neighbors, kids, sports teams, school, and so forth)

FRIENDS

FUN
(gym, hobbies, hangouts)

FIRM
(work)

GUIDE TO COMMUNION

Looking for a wonderful means of worshipping as a group? Why not lead your group in sharing the Lord's Supper? If you've never done this before, the idea certainly seems daunting, but here is a simple form by which your small group can share this sacrament. Of course, churches vary in their treatment of Communion, so you may need to adapt these suggestions to your church's beliefs.

Steps in Serving Communion

1. Out of the context of your own experience, say something brief about God's love, forgiveness, grace, mercy, commitment, tenderheartedness, or faithfulness. Connect your words with the personal stories of the group. For example, "These past few weeks, I've experienced God's mercy in the way that he untangled the situation with my son. And I've seen God show mercy to others here, too—especially to Jean and Roger." If you prefer, you can write down ahead of time what you want to say.

2. Read I Corinthians 11:23-26*: "The Lord Jesus, on the night he was betrayed, took bread, and when he had given thanks, he broke it and said, 'This is my body, which is for you; do this in remembrance of me.' In the same way, after supper he took the cup, saying, 'This cup is the new covenant in my blood; do this, whenever you drink it, in remembrance of me.' For whenever you eat this break and drink this cup, you proclaim the Lord's death until he comes."

3. Pray silently and pass the bread around the circle. While the bread is being passed, you may want to reflect quietly, sing a simple praise song, or listen to worship music.

4. When everyone has received the bread, remind them that this represents Jesus' broken body on their behalf. Simply state, "Jesus said, 'Do this in remembrance of me.' Let us eat together." Eat the bread as a group.

5. Pray silently and serve the cup. You may pass a small tray, serve people individually, or have them pick up a cup from the table.

6. When everyone has been served, remind them that the cup represents Jesus' blood that was shed for them. Simply state, "The cup of the new covenant is Jesus Christ's blood shed for you. Jesus said, 'Do this in remembrance of me.' Let us drink together." Then drink the juice as a group.

7. Conclude by singing a simple song, listening to a praise song, or having a time of prayer in thanks to God.

Practical Tips for Serving Communion

1. Prepare the elements simply, sacredly, and symbolically.

2. Be sensitive to timing in your meeting.

3. Break up pieces of cracker or soft bread on a small plate or tray. Don't use large servings of bread or grape juice. You should think about using grape juice—and not wine—because wine can cause some people to stumble.

4. Have all of the elements prepared beforehand. Then you can bring them into the room or to the table when you are ready.

*Here are some other good Communion passages: Matthew 26:26–29, Mark 14:22–25, Luke 22:14–20, I Corinthians 10:16–21, I Corinthians 11:17–34.

SMALL
GROUP
LEADERS

LEADING FOR THE FIRST TIME

Sweaty palms are a healthy sign. The Bible says that God is gracious to the humble. Remember who is in control; the time to worry is when you're not worried. Those who are soft in heart (and sweaty palmed) are those whom God is sure to speak through.

Seek support. Ask your leader, co-leader, or close friend to pray for you and prepare with you before the session. Walking through the study will help you to anticipate potentially difficult questions and discussion topics.

Bring your uniqueness to the study. Lean into who you are and how God wants you to uniquely lead the study. Prepare. Prepare. Prepare. Go through the session several times. If you are using the DVD, listen to the teaching segment and "Leader Lifter." Go to lifetogether.com and download pertinent files. Consider writing in a journal or fasting for a day to prepare yourself for what God wants to do.

Don't wait until the last minute to prepare. Ask for feedback so you can grow. Perhaps in an email or on cards handed out at the study, have everyone write down three things that you did well and one thing that you could improve on. Don't get defensive; show an openness to learn and grow.

Prayerfully consider launching a new group. This doesn't need to happen overnight, but God's heart is for this to happen over time. Not all Christians are called to be leaders or teachers, but we are all called to be "shepherds" of a few people some day.

Share with your group what God is doing in your heart. God is searching for those whose hearts are fully his. Share your trials and victories. We promise that people will relate.

Prayerfully consider to whom you would like to pass the baton next week. It's only fair. God is ready for the next member of your group to go on the faith journey that you just traveled. Make it fun and expect God to do the rest.

LEADERSHIP TRAINING 101

Congratulations! You have responded to the call to help shepherd Jesus' flock. There are few other tasks in the family of God that surpass the contribution that you will be making. As you prepare to lead (whether it is one session or the entire series), here are a few thoughts to keep in mind. We encourage you to read these and review them with each new discussion leader before he or she leads.

1. Remember that you are not alone.

God knows everything about you, and he knew that you would be asked to lead your group. Remember that it is common for all good leaders to feel that they are not ready to lead. Moses, Solomon, Jeremiah, and Timothy—they all were reluctant to lead. God promises, "Never will I leave you; never will I forsake you" (Hebrews 13:5). Whether you are leading for one evening, for several weeks or for a lifetime, you will be blessed as you serve.

2. Don't try to do it alone.

Pray right now for God to help you build a healthy leadership team. If you can enlist a co-leader to help you lead the group, you will find your experience to be much richer. This is your chance to involve as many people as you can in building a healthy group. All you have to do is call and ask people to help. You'll be surprised at the response.

3. Just be yourself. If you won't be you, who will?

God wants you to use your unique gifts and temperament. Don't try to do things exactly like another leader; do them in a way that fits you! Just admit it when you don't have an answer and apologize when you make a mistake. Your group will love you for it, and you'll sleep better at night!

4. Prepare for your meeting ahead of time.

Review the session and write down your responses to each question. Pay special attention to exercises that ask group members to do something other than engage in discussion. These exercises will help your group to live what the Bible teaches, not just talk about it. Be sure that you understand how an exercise works and bring any necessary supplies (such as paper and pens) to your meeting. If the exercise employs one of the items in the "Appendix," be sure to look over that item so you'll know how it works. Finally, review "Outline for Each Session" on pages 9–11 so that you'll remember the purpose of each section in the study.

5. Pray for your group members by name.

Before you begin your session, go around the room in your mind and pray for each member by name. You may want to review the prayer list at least once a week. Ask God to use your time together to touch the heart of every person uniquely. Expect God to lead you to whomever he wants you to encourage or challenge in a special way. If you listen, God will surely lead!

6. When you ask a question, be patient.

Someone will eventually respond. Sometimes people need a moment or two of silence to think about the question, and if silence doesn't bother you, it won't bother anyone else. After someone responds, affirm the response with a simple "thanks" or "good job." Then ask, "How about somebody else?" or "Would someone who hasn't shared like to add anything?" Be sensitive to new people or reluctant members who aren't ready to talk, pray, or do anything. If you give them a safe setting, they will blossom over time.

7. Provide transitions between questions.

When guiding the discussion, always read aloud the transitional paragraphs and the questions. Ask the group if anyone would like to read the paragraph or Bible passage. Don't call on anyone; instead, ask for a volunteer and be patient until someone begins. Be sure to thank the person who reads aloud.

8. Break into small groups each week, or they won't stay.

If your group has more than seven people, we strongly encourage you to have the group gather sometimes in discussion circles of three or four people during the "Loving God" or "Loving Others" sections of the study. With a greater opportunity to talk in a small circle, people will connect more with the study, apply more quickly what they're learning, and ultimately get more out of it. A small circle also encourages a quiet person to participate and tends to minimize the effects of a more vocal or dominant member. It can also help people in your group to feel more loved. When you gather again at the end of the section, you can have one person summarize the highlights from each circle.

Small circles are also helpful during prayer time. People who are unaccustomed to praying aloud will feel more comfortable trying it with just two or three others. Also, prayer requests won't take as much time, so circles will have more time to actually pray. When you gather back with the whole group, you can have one person from each circle briefly update everyone on the prayer requests. People are more willing to pray in small circles if they know that the whole group will hear all the prayer requests.

9. Rotate facilitators weekly.

At the end of each meeting, ask the group who should lead the following week. Let the group help select your weekly facilitator. You may be perfectly capable of leading each time, but you will help others grow in their faith and gifts if you give them opportunities to lead. You can use the "Group Calendar" on page 133 to fill in the names of all meeting leaders at once if you prefer.

10. One final challenge (for new or first-time leaders):

Before your first opportunity to lead, look up each of the five passages listed below. Read each one as a devotional exercise to help equip yourself with a shepherd's heart. Trust us on this one. If you do this, you will be more than ready for your first meeting.

Matthew 9:36	I Peter 5:2–4
Psalm 23	Ezekiel 34:11–16
I Thessalonians 2:7–8, 11–12	

HOSTING AN OPEN HOUSE

If you're starting a new group, try planning an "open house" before your first formal group meeting. Even if you only have two to four core members, it's a great way to break the ice and to consider prayerfully who else might be open to joining you over the next few weeks. You can also use this kick-off meeting to hand out study guides, spend some time getting to know each other, discuss each person's expectations for the group and briefly pray for each other.

A simple meal or good desserts always make a kick-off meeting more fun. After people introduce themselves and share how they ended up being at the meeting (you can play a game to see who has the wildest story!), have everyone respond to a few icebreaker questions: "What is your favorite family vacation?" or "What is one thing you love about your church/our community?" or "What are three things about your life growing up that most people here don't know?" Next, ask everyone to share what he or she hopes to get out of the study. You might want to review the "Small Group Agreement" on page 132 and talk about each person's expectations and priorities.

Finally, set an open chair (maybe two) in the center of your group and explain that it represents someone who would enjoy or benefit from this group but who isn't here yet. Ask people to pray about whom they could invite to join the group over the next few weeks. Hand out postcards and have everyone write an invitation or two. Don't worry about ending up with too many people; you can always have one discussion circle in the living room and another in the dining room after you watch the lesson. Each group could then report prayer requests and progress at the end of the session.

You can skip this kick-off meeting if your time is limited, but you'll experience a huge benefit if you take the time to connect with each other in this way.

The Next Seven Great Events
By Randal Ross

In this powerful biblical analysis of what is yet to come, Randal Ross reveals the next—and final—events leading to the second coming of Christ. This book of insight, conviction, and hope shows you how to recognize the signs of Christ's return and provides practical, positive direction for living in these last days.

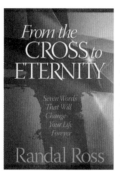

From the Cross to Eternity
By Randal Ross

Jesus' last words on the cross became defining keys to gaining victory and to understanding who he is and what the Gospel means. They lead us to the greater resurrection experience. The cross and the tomb are not the end; God is leading us to a mighty resurrection breakthrough in our lives.

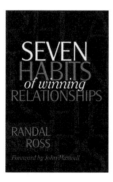

The Seven Habits of Winning Relationships
By Randal Ross

The key to finding success is in building successful relationships. Relating to others is the most important ingredient to living a life of achievement and fulfillment. Randal Ross identifies the habits that you need in order to develop winning connections with your family and friends and in business.

To purchase any of these books, contact Calvary Church:

New Day

By Ben De Boef & Michael Escamilla

When you come to faith in Jesus Christ, a new day begins. This book is for those who are just beginning their new life in God. These studies will give you direction for personal spiritual growth, help you to understand the basics of theology, and encourage you to live daily in God's purposes and blessing.

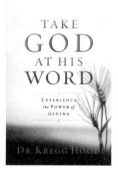

Take God at His Word

By Dr. Kregg Hood

If you've ever struggled with giving, these dynamic promises will liberate and empower you toward greater faith, ministry impact, and financial freedom. You'll learn how to experience power over fear, reject selfish temptations, and confidently place your financial future in God's strong and mighty hands.

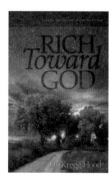

Rich Toward God

By Dr. Kregg Hood

This positive study shows Christians how to build an eternal investment portfolio that matters, regardless of one's income level! Believers will learn to trust God as the source of all blessings, put God to the test in tithing, advance God's kingdom word every day, and embrace a spirit of contentment in all areas of life.

Randal Ross has pastored churches in North Carolina and Texas, and he now pastors at Calvary Church in Naperville, Illinois. Calvary Church has worldwide impact in missions and in leadership training. Since Reverend Ross began his ministry at Calvary Church, the attendance has grown in size and diversity and currently averages 7,000 every weekend.

Reverend Ross travels throughout the world as a teacher and keynote speaker at seminars and conferences. His other books include *Tapping the Power of Your Emotions*, *Not Without My Children*, *From the Cross to Eternity*, and *The Next Seven Great Events*.

Reverend Ross and his wife, Andrea, met at Central Bible College and have a son, Matthew, who leads the web church at Calvary Church and a daughter, Jessica, who is a teacher in greater Chicagoland.

ABOUT THE AUTHOR

ADDITIONAL NOTES

_____

_____

_____

_____

_____

_____

_____

_____

_____

_____

_____

_____

_____

_____

_____

_____

_____